To my family
Neil, Robert, Chris and Liz for their
encouragement and granddaughters,
Jenna and Grace for their inspiration.
R.S.

To Sue, Cara and Lisa for always
inspiring me to do better work.
F.F.

Where does my food go?

Written by
Ruth Sundback

Illustrated by
Frank Fiorello

First Edition
10 9 8 7 6 5 4 3 2 1

Hard Cover ISBN: 978-0-9776850-1-1

Library of Congress Control Number
2007901145

Summary: Children learn that when they eat the colorful foods, they will grow to be healthy and strong

For more information,
www.sundbackbooks.com

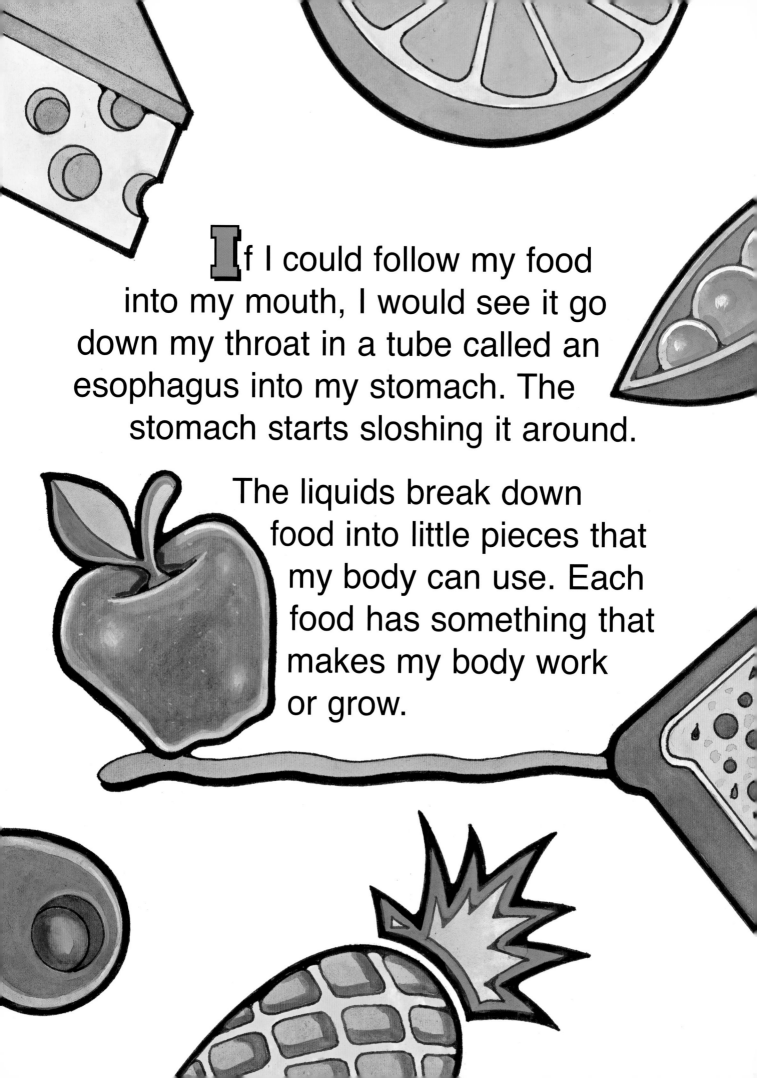

If I could follow my food into my mouth, I would see it go down my throat in a tube called an esophagus into my stomach. The stomach starts sloshing it around.

The liquids break down food into little pieces that my body can use. Each food has something that makes my body work or grow.

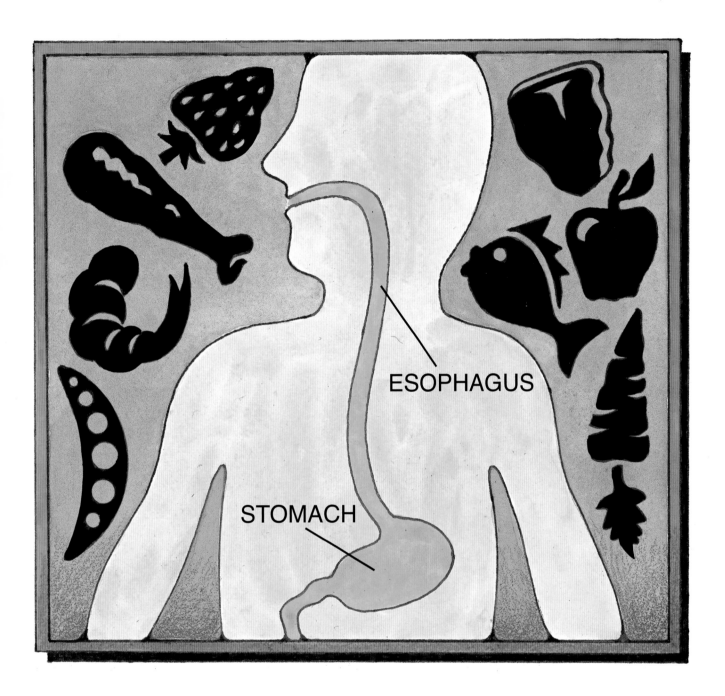

So, let's see!
Where does my food go?

I like **Milk.**

It has calcium and phosphorus.
It helps make teeth and bones.

See my teeth. I feel my bones
under my skin - fingers, toes, legs.

Calcium helps my heart beat.
I can feel my heart beat.

Where does milk go?

I like
Juice, **O**ranges and **S**trawberries.

They have vitamin **C**.
This helps heal my cuts
and may help me from
catching colds.

 # Where does juice go?

I like **Carrots** & **Cantaloupe**

They have vitamin 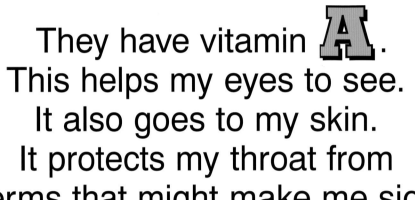.
This helps my eyes to see.
It also goes to my skin.
It protects my throat from
germs that might make me sick.

Where
do
carrots
go?

I like **Chicken, Hamburger & Beans.**

They give me protein.
This helps me grow and
gives me muscles.
Feel my arm muscle!

I like  **Eggs, Meat, Spinach & Raisins**

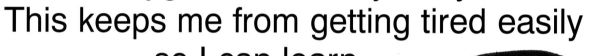

They give me minerals
like zinc & iron.
Zinc helps me to taste all food and helps
heal cuts and sores.
Iron makes my blood red and carries
oxygen all over my body.
This keeps me from getting tired easily
so I can learn.

Where does an egg go?

I like **Bread, Cereal, Rice & Spaghetti.**

They give me calories and
energy to play and grow.
They also give me vitamin **B**
that helps my brain and nerves.
Nerves are like little strings inside
the skin that lead to the brain.
They help me feel, taste,
hear, see and smell.

Where does bread go?

I like
Butter, Cream Cheese
& Salad Dressing.

They make my food taste good.
They give me fat that gives
me energy to play.
They also carry some vitamins to
my skin and other parts of my body.

 # Where does butter go?

I like **Salads, Peas, Corn, Apples** & **Bananas.**

They give me lots of vitamins and minerals. They also give me fiber, which helps food move through the body. It helps me go to the bathroom and not get constipated.

Where do fruits & vegetables go?

I drink lots of WateR

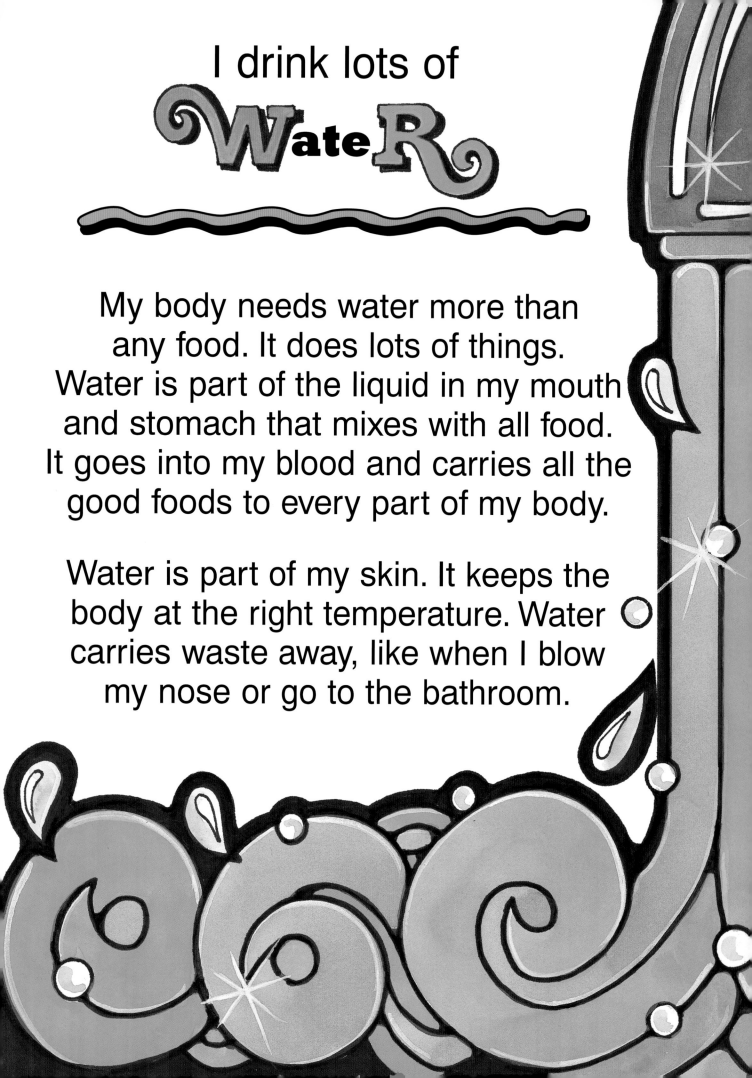

My body needs water more than any food. It does lots of things. Water is part of the liquid in my mouth and stomach that mixes with all food. It goes into my blood and carries all the good foods to every part of my body.

Water is part of my skin. It keeps the body at the right temperature. Water carries waste away, like when I blow my nose or go to the bathroom.

Where does water go?

What if I eat
candy, cookies, cake
and fried foods and
drink soda pop?

These foods have lots of
calories but don't make
my body work as well
as all the colorful
foods.

If I eat the

COLORFUL

foods first, I will
grow to be healthy
and strong.

Where does my food go?

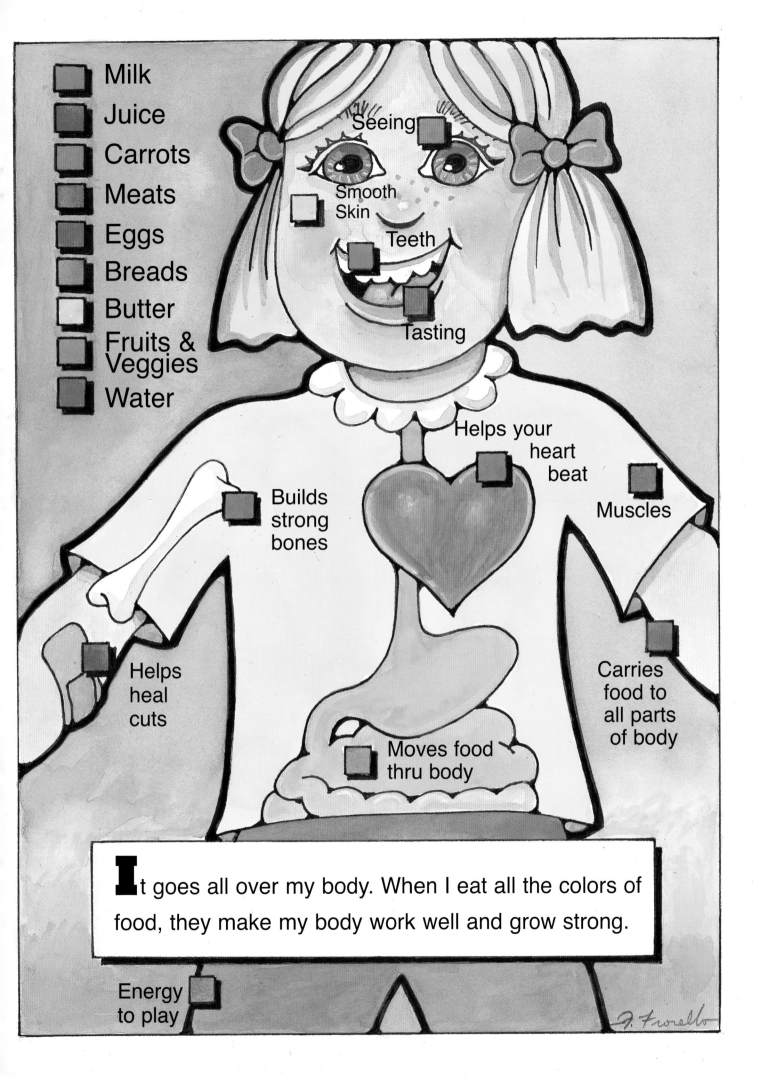

Activities

★ Eat **4** or more colors at each meal. Count the colors.

★ Draw a plate of food that you ate. How many colors? What foods could add color.

On a trip to the grocery store,

Make it a yellow day (or red or green or blue/purple day). Name all yellow fruits and vegetables. Pick out one to buy and try.

Don't like some foods?

Our tastes change as we grow older, so keep trying new foods. Surprise Mom by trying one small spoon of a new food. If you don't like it, try it again next month. Soon, you will like it.

How much of all the foods do we need daily?

FOOD		*SERVING SIZE

MILK 2-3 servings

1 cup milk or yogurt,
1 oz. cheese

FRUITS & VEGETABLES
4-7 servings

1/2 cup juice, 1piece
or 1/2 cup fruit/vegetables

Vitamin C food – 1/2 cup a day
Citrus fruits or strawberries

Vitamin A food – 1/2 cup every other day
Green or orange vegetables or fruits

MEAT/PROTEIN
2 servings

2-3 oz. meat/fish, 2 tbsp.
peanut butter, 1/2 cup beans

STARCHES
7-10 servings

1 slice bread or tortilla,
1/2 cup pasta, rice, cereal,
5-8 crackers

FATS
3-6 servings

1 tsp. Butter or oil, 10 olives,
1 tbsp. Cream cheese

WATER
Amount varies.

For adults & children (not toddlers),
drink half your body weight in ounces.
Example: 50 lbs. divided by 2 will equal
25 ounces of water. The total can include
some juice and milk. Hot weather and
exercise increase water need.

---

*Toddler serving sizes are 1 tbsp. of solid food item per year old, minimum. Example: 3 year old child's portion is 3 tbsp. each of vegetable, fruit, meat or cereal. For infant's diet and serving size, follow the doctor's recommendation.

Sample menu & snacks

BREAKFAST
cheerios with milk,
toast with butter,
orange juice

SNACK
fruit or yogurt

LUNCH
chicken soup with rice,
carrots, crackers and
cheese, milk

SNACK
bugs on a log

DINNER
spaghetti with meat sauce,
green salad with dressing,
Italian bread with butter,
juice, milk or water

SNACK
apples dipped in
peanut butter

Easy Recipes for kids

BUGS ON A LOG
celery sticks
cream cheese or peanut butter
raisins

Clean celery, Cut into 2 inch pieces. Spread with peanut butter or
cream cheese. Add raisins on top. Enjoy!

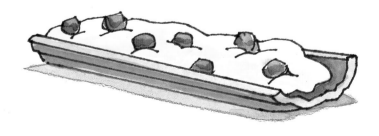

SIMPLE SOUP
1 can of chicken broth, 1/2 cup of cut up carrots
and celery (and any other vegetable you want
to try, especially the new veggie you got at the
grocery store). Heat broth in a pan. Add veggies
and simmer until soft. Optional: Add 1 cup cooked
pasta or rice and 1/2 cup cooked meat (chicken or
chopped beef) Enjoy!

Match Game

Draw a line from the foods in column **A** to WHERE THE FOOD GOES in column **B**.

A

Milk

Orange Juice

Chicken

Broccoli

Carrots

Bread

Cereal

Eggs and Shrimp

Butter

Olives

Water

Apple   Corn

B

Builds Muscle

Strong Teeth

Good Eyes

Taste Food

Heals Cuts

Energy to Play

Smooth Skin

Helps Food Move

Controls Temperature